J979 WB

EARLY PEOPLES

INDIANS OF THE SOUTHWEST

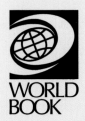

WORLD
BOOK

World Book
a Scott Fetzer company
Chicago
www.worldbookonline.com

World Book, Inc.
233 N. Michigan Avenue
Chicago, IL 60601
U.S.A.

For information about other World Book publications, visit our
Web site at http://www.worldbookonline.com or call
1-800-WORLDBK (967-5325).
For information about sales to schools and libraries, call
1-800-975-3250 (United States), or 1-800-837-5365 (Canada).

Library of Congress Cataloging-in-Publication Data

Indians of the Southwest.
    p. cm. -- (Early peoples)
  Includes index.
  Summary: "A discussion of the Indians of the Southwest, including
who they were, where they lived, the rise of civilization, social structure,
religion, art and architecture, science and technology, daily life,
entertainment and sports, and fall of civilization. Features include
timelines, fact boxes, glossary, list of recommended reading and Web sites,
and index"--Provided by publisher.
  ISBN 978-0-7166-2142-3
  1. Indians of North America--Southwest, New--History--Juvenile
literature. 2. Indians of North America--Southwest, New--Social life
and customs--Juvenile literature. 3. Southwest, New--History--Juvenile
literature. 4. Southwest, New--Social life and customs--Juvenile literature.
I. World Book, Inc.
  E78.S7.I453 2009
  979--dc22
                                        2008024159

Printed in China by Leo Paper Products Ltd.,
Heshan, Guangdong
2nd printing June 2010

STAFF

EXECUTIVE COMMITTEE
President
  Paul A. Gazzolo
Vice President and Chief Marketing Officer
  Patricia Ginnis
Vice President and Chief Financial Officer
  Donald D. Keller
Vice President and Editor in Chief
  Paul A. Kobasa
Director, Human Resources
  Bev Ecker
Chief Technology Officer
  Tim Hardy
Managing Director, International
  Benjamin Hinton

EDITORIAL
Editor in Chief
  Paul A. Kobasa
Associate Director, Supplementary
Publications
  Scott Thomas
Managing Editor, Supplementary
Publications
  Barbara A. Mayes
Senior Editor, Supplementary Publications
  Kristina Vaicikonis
Manager, Research, Supplementary
Publications
  Cheryl Graham
Manager, Contracts & Compliance
  (Rights & Permissions)
  Loranne K. Shields

Administrative Assistant
  Ethel Matthews
Editors
  Nicholas Kilzer
  Scott Richardson
  Christine Sullivan

GRAPHICS AND DESIGN
Associate Director
  Sandra M. Dyrlund
Manager
  Tom Evans
Coordinator, Design Development and
Production
  Brenda B. Tropinski

EDITORIAL ADMINISTRATION
Director, Systems and Projects
  Tony Tills
Senior Manager, Publishing Operations
  Timothy Falk

PRODUCTION
Director, Manufacturing and Pre-Press
  Carma Fazio
Manufacturing Manager
  Steve Hueppchen
Production/Technology Manager
  Anne Fritzinger
Production Specialist
  Curley Hunter
Proofreader
  Emilie Schrage

MARKETING
Chief Marketing Officer
  Patricia Ginnis
Associate Director, School and Library
Marketing
  Jennifer Parello

Produced for World Book by
  White-Thomson Publishing Ltd.
  +44 (0)845 362 8240
  www.wtpub.co.uk
Steve White-Thomson, President

Writer: Stephanie Fitzgerald
Editors: Valerie Weber, Robert Famighetti
Designer: Clare Nicholas
Photo Researcher: Amy Sparks
Map Artist: Stefan Chabluk
Illustrator: Adam Hook (p. 28)
Fact Checker: Charlene Rimsa
Proofreader: Catherine Gardner
Indexer: Nila Glikin

Consultant:
Donald L. Birchfield
Professor of Native American Studies
University of Lethbridge
Lethbridge, Alberta, Canada

TABLE OF CONTENTS

Glossary There is a glossary on pages 60-61. Terms defined in the glossary are in type **that looks like this** on their first appearance on any spread (two facing pages).

Additional Resources Books for further reading and recommended Web sites are listed on page 62. Because of the nature of the Internet, some Web site addresses may have changed since publication. The publisher has no responsibility for any such changes or for the content of cited sources.

WHO WERE THE ANCIENT INDIANS OF THE SOUTHWEST?

The ancient Indians of the Southwest had complex and sophisticated **cultures**. They adapted their ways of life to suit the lands they called home—some of the harshest desert environments in the United States. Along the way, these early peoples created beautiful and often mysterious works of art. They also constructed highly advanced **irrigation** systems and sprawling housing complexes using little more than the simplest tools. What remains of these cultures, including the architectural wonders they left behind, continues to fascinate people to this day.

Scientists believe that people have lived in the southwestern part of what is now the United States for more than 13,000 years. The first people to live in this area are called **Paleo-Indians** by **archaeologists**. Many Indians living today, however, believe that their ancestors have always lived in North America.

A Changing Way of Life

The Paleo-Indians' way of life changed dramatically during the time they lived in the Southwest. Originally, they hunted such large animals as giant bison, mammoths, and mastodons. But by 10,000 years ago,

▼ The Southwest region of the United States is a harsh environment. Water is scarce, and few plants and animals in the region can be eaten by humans. The Indians who lived in this region had to learn how to make the most of what little natural resources were available to them.

these animals had become scarce. Scientists are not sure what happened to the animals. Some believe that a combination of over-hunting and climate change may have been to blame for their dying out. As the Paleo-Indians' food source disappeared, to avoid starvation, they began concentrating on smaller game. They hunted; fished; and gathered nuts, berries, and other plants. The change in diet marked the beginning of a new era. Archaeologists named this new era the *Archaic (ahr KAY ihk) Period*. Archaic people were **nomadic**—they had to move from place to place in search of food. They traveled in small bands and usually lived in caves or temporary camps.

THE POINT OF THE NAME

Archaeologists named Paleo-Indian groups based on the areas where their **artifacts** were discovered. Artifacts include weapons, tools, and other items made and used by people. The names of these groups include Clovis (*KLOH vihs*), Folsom (*FOL suhm*), and Sandia (*san DEE uh*). These groups all made uniquely-shaped spear points (a Folsom spear point is shown here). These points were strong enough to pierce the tough hide of a mammoth. Hunting animals as large as mammoths must have been difficult for the Paleo-Indians. Experts believe that groups of hunters went after a single animal.

The Archaic people's way of life changed significantly again about 4,000 years ago when they started planting corn. Corn was first cultivated in Mexico. **Hunter-gatherers** from Mexico probably carried corn seeds with them as they traveled into the Southwest region.

Once the Archaic people began farming, they no longer needed to move from place to place to find food. They could build more permanent homes. Because there was more food available through farming, more people could live together in one place. These conditions led to the rise of new cultures in the deserts of the Southwest.

THE ANCESTRAL PUEBLOANS AND WHERE THEY LIVED

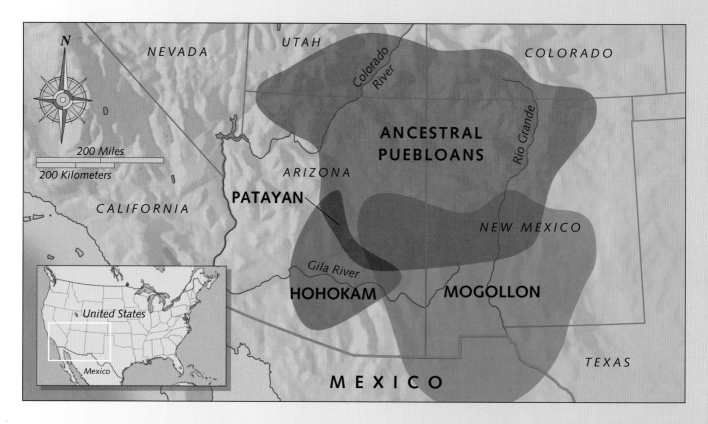

▲ The ancient Indians of the Southwest lived mainly in an area that is today referred to as the Four Corners region. It is the only place in the United States where four states—Arizona, Colorado, New Mexico, and Utah—meet. A monument marks the site, which is a popular tourist attraction.

Archaeologists usually call the time after the Archaic Period the *Formative Period.* This period began about 4,000 years ago. The Southwest Indian groups from the Formative Period include the Ancestral Puebloans (also known as Anasazi), Mogollon, Hohokam, and Patayan. They occupied overlapping territories in what is now known as the Four Corners region of the southwestern United States. Although some groups ranged as far south as northern Mexico and as far west as California, the people mainly lived in what are now the states of Arizona, Colorado, New Mexico, and Utah.

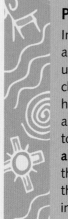

PROTECTING THE PAST

In 1888, a rancher named Richard Wetherill stumbled across the ruins at **Mesa** Verde, a previously undocumented group of enormous Ancestral Puebloan cliff dwellings. Wetherill became known as a "pot hunter" in scientific circles because he discovered—and sold—many ancient Indian **artifacts**. In an effort to stop people like Wetherill from taking things from **archaeological** sites, the United States Congress passed the American Antiquities Act in 1906. The act allowed the government to protect public lands and was crucial in preserving important ancient sites.

The Ancient Ones

Anasazi *(AH nuh SAH zee)* is a name that has been used for the ancestors of Pueblo Indians. Modern Pueblo prefer the terms "Ancestral Puebloans" or "Hisatsinom" *(hih SAHT sih nohm)* to describe their ancestors. Anasazi is a Navajo Indian word meaning *enemy of long ago*.

Archaeologists refer to the early Ancestral Puebloans *(PWEHB loh uhnz)* as Basketmakers (500 B.C.-A.D. 800) because of their great skill at weaving baskets. (The later introduction of ceramic pottery resulted in the decline of basketmaking.) Ancestral Puebloans who lived during the period when they constructed buildings called **pueblos** *(PWEHB lohz)* are referred to as Pueblo (A.D. 800-1300). The Basketmaker and Pueblo phases are further broken down into different stages of development.

The region occupied by the Ancestral Puebloans covered northeastern Arizona, northwestern New Mexico, southeastern Utah, and southwestern Colorado. The most famous Ancestral Puebloan settlements are found in Chaco Canyon in New Mexico and at Mesa Verde *(MAY suh vurd* or *MAY suh VUR dee)* in Colorado.

▲ The Cliff Palace at Mesa Verde National Park in Colorado is one of the best-known ancient settlements in the world. The Ancestral Puebloans built the settlement using hand-shaped sandstone blocks. They used soil, water, and ash to make the mortar in between the blocks, then added pieces of stone (called chinking stones) to fill in gaps. The Cliff Palace is one of several cliff houses at Mesa Verde and is the largest cliff dwelling in North America. It contains more than 150 living rooms.

THE MOGOLLON, HOHOKAM, AND PATAYAN AND WHERE THEY LIVED

The Pottery Makers

The Mogollon *(moh guh YOHN)* group of Southwest Indians was named after the region in which they lived—the Mogollon Mountains in western New Mexico. They extend into east-central and southeastern Arizona and northern Mexico. Although the Mogollon territory included low-lying deserts, the Mogollon were primarily mountain people. The Mogollon's development is usually divided into three phases named for the shelters that they built: Early Pit House (A.D. 200-600), Late Pit House (A.D. 600-1150), and Mogollon Pueblo (A.D. 1150-1400). A **pit house** is an ancient type of shelter that is built over a hole in the ground.

A Hohokam pottery dish found in the 1930's at Snaketown, an important Hohokam settlement located near present-day Phoenix, Arizona. Experts estimate that the dish was crafted sometime around A.D. 500-900. Hundreds of such pieces of pottery have been found at Snaketown.

The Vanished Ones

Some scientists believe the Hohokam *(huh HOH kuhm)* Indians **migrated** north from Mexico around 300 B.C. Over time, these ancient farmers brought the desert under cultivation and created magnificent art. The Hohokam were given their name, which means *the vanished ones,* by the Pima *(PEE muh)* Indians, who still live in the southwestern United States. **Archaeologists** divide Hohokam history into four phases: Pioneer (A.D. 300-550), Colonial (A.D. 550-900), Sedentary (A.D. 900-1100), and Classic (A.D. 1100-1450).

The Hohokam lived near the Salt and Gila rivers in the Sonoran Desert of southern Arizona. By redirecting water from the rivers into their fields, the Hohokam were able to farm in the desert. They

▲ Mogollon tools made of animal bones. Like other ancient peoples, the Mogollon used nearly every part of the animals they hunted; they did not just eat the meat and throw the rest away.

also hunted and collected plants in the dry, low-lying area of the Sonoran Desert and the surrounding foothills.

The Old People

Less is known about the Patayan (*puh-TY-uhn*) people than about the other Southwest Indian groups. The Patayan (A.D. 700-1500) remained heavily reliant on hunting and gathering to supplement their crops. Because people who lived by hunting and gathering generally moved around a lot, they usually crafted lightweight **artifacts**. Lightweight objects break down and disappear over time. Without artifacts to study, scientists have a harder time figuring out how the Patayan lived. *Patayan* is a Yuma Indian word that means *old people*. The Yuma were a later Indian group who lived in the same region.

The Patayan lived in the western part of the Sonoran Desert in Arizona. They were able to survive in this incredibly hot, dry area by hunting small animals, gathering desert plants, and farming along the Colorado River. After the river rose, flooded, and subsided (lowered), the Patayan would plant crops in the silt (fine particles of earth, sand, clay, or similar matter carried by moving water) that was left behind.

MARKING TIME

Archaeologists have given dates to the different eras of ancient Indian **cultures**, such as the pioneer phase of the Hohokam. These dates, however, are just estimates. Cultures do not completely change overnight. Change generally takes place over a period of time. Although experts cannot give specific start and end dates to these eras, they can assign precise dates to the artifacts they study.

LIVING OFF THE LAND

Ancient Indians survived by making the most of their surroundings. Because each group's territory contained a variety of habitats, the group did not have to rely on one method of getting food.

Desert Dwellers

The Sonoran Desert, home to the Patayan and Hohokam, includes land in Arizona and Colorado, as well as part of the Mexican state of Sonora and the Baja California peninsula in Mexico. The Patayan planted crops by the river when rain was plentiful and the river was high. They moved into the mountains to hunt and gather when water was scarce.

The Hohokam built **irrigation** systems to water their crops to guarantee a more reliable source of food. They also continued to hunt and gather. The most important Hohokam settlement that has been **excavated** is called Snaketown, located near present-day Phoenix, Arizona. **Archaeologists** found many **artifacts,** including decorated bowls and stone tools, at Snaketown that helped shape their theories about the Hohokam.

◀ Mogollon projectile points discovered near present-day Truth or Consequences, New Mexico. The artifacts, which are made of flint, could have been used as the tips of arrows or spears. Although the Mogollon planted crops in small plots, they remained **hunter-gatherers.**

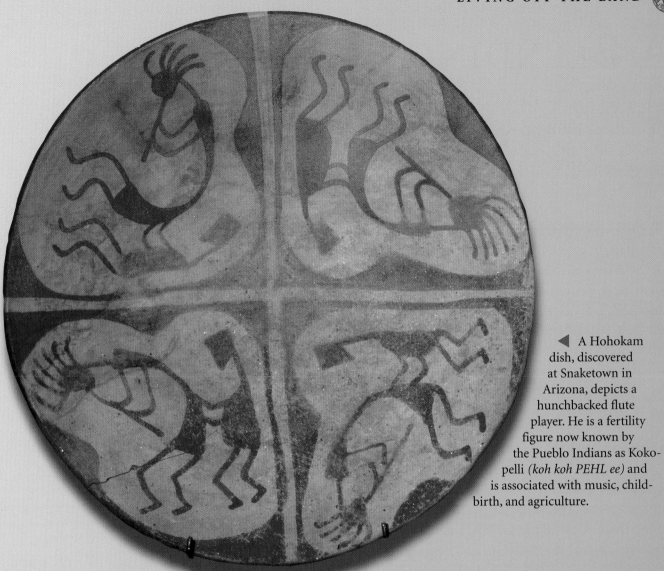

◀ A Hohokam
dish, discovered
at Snaketown in
Arizona, depicts a
hunchbacked flute
player. He is a fertility
figure now known by
the Pueblo Indians as Kokopelli *(koh koh PEHL ee)* and
is associated with music, child-
birth, and agriculture.

Highland People

The Mogollon planted small farm plots and took whatever else they needed from the land. Nearby mountains and desert valleys would have provided the Mogollon with berries, nuts, and seeds, as well as game.

Two Mogollon sites in Arizona, Bluff Village and Bear Village, provided scientists with clues about how the people lived during the Early (A.D. 200-600) and Late (600-1150) Pit House phases. The Chodistaas (*choh DIHS tahs*) and Grasshopper Pueblos, also in Arizona, provide information about the Pueblo period of Mogollon life (1150-1400). In each case, archaeologists could tell how the people built their dwellings—and how they used the space. If a researcher found a lot of tools in one of the rooms of a pueblo, for example, he or she could safely assume the room was used as a workroom.

Many archaeological finds, such as those at **Mesa** Verde, have provided information about how the Ancestral Puebloans lived. Although Mesa Verde is associated with its cliff dwellings, the area also includes villages from the Ancestral Puebloans' earliest days. From these villages, experts can estimate how long the Mesa Verdeans lived in **pit houses** and at about what time they moved to cliff dwellings.

A BLENDING OF CULTURES

Archaeological evidence reveals that the ancient Indians of the Southwest traded with distant tribes as well as with each other. They also often shared artistic ideas and techniques with their neighbors.

Ancient Traders

Archaeologists believe the Hohokam traded heavily with other Southwestern groups and with people from the West Coast of North America and Mesoamerica (Mexico and Central America). The raw materials they used to create rings, bracelets, pendants, and other **ornaments** made from shells, for example, came from the Pacific Coast. The Hohokam then traded the finished jewelry and ornaments with various tribes. They also acquired copper bells from Mesoamerica, which they traded with their neighbors.

The Ancestral Puebloans likely obtained cotton by trade. They wove the cotton into beautiful textiles. They were also famous for the blankets that they made from turkey feathers woven into **yucca cordage**. Scientists speculate that they probably traded these goods for the shells, beads, and macaw feathers they used to decorate clothing and items used in ceremonies.

MAKING MUSIC

Scientists believe that Southwestern Indians attached copper bells—made in Mesoamerica and acquired through trade—to their clothes to provide part of the rhythm for ceremonial dancing. During the same period, many Mesoamerican Indian tribes sewed bells onto their ceremonial costumes—and still do.

▼ Many pieces of Hohokam pottery are decorated with red paint on a buff background. The zigzag lines and animal motifs used on three of the plates shown here are similar to those used by other Indian groups, indicating a sharing of styles. The flowered dish, on the other hand, is very unusual.

Sharing Ideas

Goods were not the only things traded among the Southwestern tribes. Members of one tribe sometimes married into another tribe. At times, whole families from one group joined the village of another. When two **cultures** live together, each group usually adopts some of the ways of the other. At the Mogollon settlement at Bear Village, in Arizona, archaeologists have found the remains of many Ancestral Puebloans buried with those of the Mogollon. They could tell the difference between the two groups based on the shapes of their skulls. The remains of the shelters that were found showed design features of both the Mogollon and the Ancestral Puebloans.

Archaeologists who **excavated** the Mogollon Tla Kii *(tlah kee)* Ruin in the Forestdale Valley in Arizona found pottery similar to that made by their Ancestral Puebloan neighbors. This discovery suggests that the Mogollon people who lived at Tla Kii adopted the pottery style used by their neighbors. It is also possible that nearby Ancestral Puebloans left their villages to live at Tla Kii.

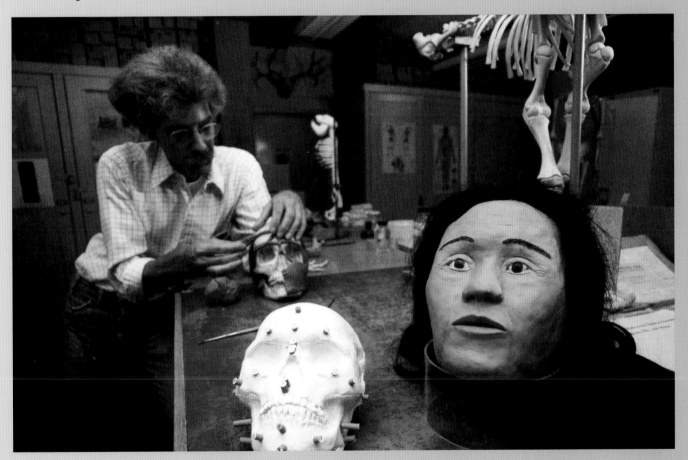

▲ A forensic artist recreates what an Ancestral Puebloan may have looked like by making a cast of an ancient skull and adding clay "muscles," "skin," and other facial features. Archaeologists can identify what tribe a person belonged to based on the shape of a skull.

PREHISTORIC SOCIETIES

Archaeologists have no way of knowing exactly how ancient people lived because they left no written records. However, studying the lives of these people's descendants provides clues as to how the ancient ones might have lived.

Tracing Their Roots

Most modern Pueblo groups are organized into extended family groups called **clans.** Clan membership is traced through females in what is called a **matrilineal** (MAT *ruh LIHN ee uhl*) system. When a man and a woman get married, the husband goes to live with his wife's family. The couple's children belong to their mother's clan. Because their descendants are organized in a matrilineal system, experts believe the Ancestral Puebloans were too.

The Pima and Tohono O'odham (*toh HOH noh OH uh dahm* or *toh HOH noh oh OH duhm*) are descendants of the Hohokam. Because these groups are organized in a **patrilineal** (PAT *ruh LIHN ee uhl*) system, scientists can assume that the Hohokam were organized in the same way. In a patrilineal system, membership in a family group is traced through the father's side.

◀ Casa Grande National Monument in Arizona preserves the remains of an ancient Hohokam settlement that was one of the largest prehistoric structures ever built in North America. Archaeologists believe the Hohokam abandoned the site around A.D. 1450. Such sites provide scientists with clues of how ancient people may have lived.

Social Standing

Archaeological evidence provides no clues as to how the Ancestral Puebloans picked their leaders. It does, however, offer a glimpse at how they cared for one another. Archaeologists have discovered the remains of a good number of Ancestral Puebloans. Many were old or physically disabled—that is, people who were unlikely to have been able to provide for themselves. Archaeologists believe that they were probably cared for by other people in the community.

Scientists believe that the Mogollon also showed great respect for their elders. Evidence of this is found in burial sites. Older people in this community were buried with more **artifacts** than younger people. Also, men were usually buried with more items than women. This suggests that the Mogollon men had more power than the women.

Because the homes in Hohokam villages all seem to have been about the same size and quality, scientists believe the Hohokam lived as equals. Unfortunately, scientists have been unable to determine under what system the Patayan were organized.

▶ A Mogollon pottery bowl that was buried with a body as an offering. Archaeologists believe the hole might have been made in the dish as part of a ceremony in which the item was ritually "killed" to join its owner.

RESPECT FOR THE DEAD

For archaeologists, opening graves of early Indians, such as the Ancestral Puebloans, is often necessary for understanding their cultures. However, many modern American Indians regard this practice as disrespectful and are opposed to museum displays of skeletons and objects they consider holy. The Native American Graves Protection and Repatriation Act of 1990 established a process by which these objects can be returned to tribes that have a valid claim to them. Many museums, including the Peabody Museum of Archaeology and Ethnology at Harvard University in Cambridge, Massachusetts; and the National Museum of Natural History in Washington, D.C.; have removed skeletons, ceremonial goods, and other items excavated from Ancestral Puebloan, Pueblo, and other Indian sites and returned them to descendent tribes.

THE ROLES OF MEN AND WOMEN

Much of what scientists believe about the roles of men and women in the ancient Southwest is based on how later American Indian tribes divided labor. Other theories are based on the **artifacts** that have been found in burial chambers.

Men's Work

Sometimes entire villages were involved in a hunt. Early Ancestral Puebloans and Hohokam used teamwork to drive rabbits and other small animals into nets. Most hunting—especially for larger game—was probably done by men and older boys.

Scientists believe that men probably also helped plant crops, build houses, and in the case of the Hohokam, dig the **irrigation** canals that carried water from rivers and streams onto fields. Because the ancient Indians used only sharpened sticks for the job, digging was especially hard work. They used baskets to carry away the dirt.

Scientists also believe that men were in charge of religious ceremonies. **Archaeologists** base this idea on the artifacts, including **sacred** objects, that are often only found buried with the

▼ Ancestral Puebloan men, whom scientists believe were in charge of religious ceremonies, used a wooden ladder to reach the sacred kiva underground. (The roof of the kiva doubled as the floor of the community plaza.) Men used kivas for religious **rituals** and to teach young boys about special sacred societies.

TRADING PLACES

Archaeologists believe that men sometimes did "women's work," especially when it related to ceremonial or trade items. Hohokam men often made jewelry, for example. Scientists uncovered evidence of a **loom** in an Ancestral Puebloan site. Holes in the floor of a **kiva** *(KEE vuh)* showed where the posts for an upright loom had been placed. Kivas, religious meeting places and ceremonial structures, were used only by men during the Pueblo phase of Ancestral Puebloan **culture**.

remains of males. At Grasshopper **Pueblo** in Arizona, burial sites revealed that about half of the adult men were buried with artifacts associated with ceremonial roles.

A Woman's World

Although men probably skinned and gutted game at the kill site, women most likely cut up the meat and cooked it. They also preserved the meat by slicing it into thin strips and hanging it up to dry in the sun or to smoke over a fire. The women probably also scraped and cleaned the animal hides so they could be used for clothing.

It is also likely that women harvested the crops, gathered such wild foods as berries and nuts, and prepared the food. Archaeologists believe women wove plant fibers into baskets, sandals, cords, and other useful items. Because pottery was crafted primarily for everyday use, it was probably created by the woman who used it.

◀ A pot and earrings testify to the Ancestral Puebloans' love of beauty. Archaeologists believe both pieces would have been crafted and used by the women of the group.

THE SPIRIT WORLD

Scientists believe that the ancient Indians of the Southwest were highly spiritual. They base that assumption on the artwork the people left behind, the ceremonial structures found throughout their ruins, and the way they treated their dead.

Ceremonial Structures

The **kiva** was an important religious ceremonial structure that was used by many ancient Indians of the Southwest in the later phases of their **cultures**. These rooms were used by holy men and religious societies for meetings and ceremonies. Kivas were often built totally or partially underground.

A typical underground kiva was round, with walls lined with stones. The ground above served as a roof. A ladder, which passed through a hole in the roof, was the only entrance and exit. A hole in the wall led to a shaft that allowed air to circulate through the structure. The interior was centered on a fire pit. Next to the fire pit, a stone or stones protected the fire from the air that came in from the shaft and kept the fire from blowing out.

▼ The largest of the Great Kivas at **Pueblo** Bonito in the Chaco Canyon National Historic Monument in New Mexico is 16 feet (5 meters) deep and 70 feet (21 meters) in diameter. Originally, it would have been roofed over at ground level. Scientists believe that the square niches in the walls may have been used to house **sacred** or ceremonial objects.

Most kivas contained a bench that ran along the walls. Perhaps most importantly, the kiva contained a **sipapu** *(SEE pah poo)*, an opening in the floor through which **supernatural** beings were believed to enter during ceremonies.

The Hohokam used platform mounds for public ceremonies. The platform mounds from the Classic Period (about A.D. 1150) were rectangular and looked like pyramids with the tops cut off. A wall enclosed each mound and open areas on the ground, which scientists speculate may have provided space for spectators.

Honoring the Dead

The care with which ancient Indians treated their dead reveals their deep concern for the afterlife, or life after death. Mogollon people and Ancestral Puebloans buried their dead, fully dressed, with offerings of baskets, ceremonial objects, weapons, and tools.

After a Hohokam person died, he or she was dressed in fine clothing and jewelry and placed on a platform over a pit filled with wood. More wood was then piled on the body, and the platform was set on fire. The ashes were later placed in a pottery vessel and buried. The person's possessions, ceremonial objects, and offerings were usually placed with the ashes in the burial pit or buried next to it.

▲ The kiva at **Mesa** Verde in Colorado displays many features common to kivas: a fire pit; an air shaft; stones to block drafts; and a sipapu, an opening in the floor through which supernatural beings were believed to enter. According to a Hopi legend of creation, the Pueblo's ancestors lived in three dark underworlds. In their search for light, the spirits of the dead climbed a spruce tree into this world. The sipapu was the opening through which they emerged.

PREHISTORIC RITUALS AND CEREMONIES

The spiritual world probably played a large role in the daily lives of the ancient Indians of the Southwest, as it did for their descendants. No doubt they relied on special **rituals** to ensure their well-being. A ritual is a certain series of actions carried out for religious or social reasons.

A Natural Balance

As people of the land, ancient Indians probably tried to stay in harmony with the natural world. It is likely that their ceremonies and rituals centered on the basics of life: bringing rain, ensuring a successful harvest or hunt, curing the sick, and burying the dead.

Every village had different ceremonial groups. Each group was in charge of a certain area of life. For example, there might be one group that was concerned only with rain, or one that dealt with hunting. Each of these groups had its own **kiva** and leader or holy man. However, there was probably also one holy man in charge of the spiritual life of the entire village.

Based upon the existence of copper bells uncovered at ancient sites, **archaeologists** believe that dance was an important part of ancient Indian rituals. Further evidence of the importance of dance was found in the Great Kiva at Grasshopper Ruin in Arizona, where archaeologists

▲ A wall painting in an Ancestral Puebloan kiva. The painting depicts a pottery bowl filled with offerings for the spirits. Presenting offerings to **supernatural** beings was an important part of many rituals.

▲ An archaeologist **excavates** an Ancestral Puebloan kiva near Mesa Verde National Park in Colorado. Scientists can determine when these structures were last used by studying charcoal samples found in the fire pits.

discovered a foot drum. The drum was made by digging a trench in the floor, lining it with stones, and laying wooden planks or logs across the top. Archaeologists believe that the wooden planks made a rumbling sound like thunder when Mogollon dancers struck them with their feet. On the floor of the kiva, scientists also found a **metate** *(may TAH tay)*, a rough stone with a flat or bowl-shaped surface that was used for grinding white clay. The existence of a metate suggests that the ancient people painted their faces and bodies for ceremonies.

At Mogollon, Hohokam, and Ancestral Puebloan sites, scientists have discovered ceremonial carved figurines, ceremonial pipes, and prayer sticks, which are called **pahos**. A paho is usually carved from wood and is often decorated with feathers, turquoise, and carved figures.

SACRED PLANTS

Archaeologists have discovered objects that have led them to conclude that Mogollon and Ancestral Puebloan holy men consumed certain plants and mushrooms to put themselves into a sort of trance. Mogollon prayer sticks have been unearthed that feature carvings of mushrooms that produce hallucinations when eaten. Seeds from a datura plant, which also affects the mind, were found in a kiva at **Mesa** Verde.

Sky Watchers

For ancient Indians, tracking the passage of the seasons was a matter of life and death. According to **archaeologists**, some ruins provide evidence that the Indians of the Southwest, like most ancient peoples, tracked the seasons by carefully watching the skies.

Ancient Astronomers

The Sun Dagger at Chaco Canyon in Arizona is a famous ancient solar calendar. It marks the **solstices** and **equinoxes**. Solstices are the two times of the year when the sun is at either its northernmost or southernmost position. Equinoxes are the two times of the year when the sun is directly above Earth's equator. From these four days of the year, ancient people could calculate when to plant and harvest crops and, probably, when hunting would likely be most successful.

In Chaco Canyon, three slabs of sandstone lean against a rock wall near the top of a lone hill called Fajada Butte. Inside the shaded area created by the slabs are two spiral rock carvings called **petroglyphs** *(PEHT ruh glihfz)*. During the solstices and equinoxes, rays of sunlight (or "daggers") shine through the openings in the slabs and pass across the petroglyphs in varying patterns. For example, during the spring and fall equinoxes, a sunray cuts into a

◄ Hovenweep, on the border of Colorado and Utah, is an Ancestral Puebloan ruin. Hovenweep Castle, one of the structures at the site, is an observatory. The openings in the building operate as a solar calendar— light falls at specific points in the building on the solstices and equinoxes.

▲ Sunlight passing through the spaces between slabs of rock on the solar calendar at Chaco Canyon marks the winter solstice. The Ancestral Puebloans created an accurate solar calendar at the top of Fajada Butte. (A butte is an isolated flat-topped hill.) Sunlight passing through the spaces forms "sun daggers" that hit spiral rock carvings in different places at different times of year. Here, the two daggers at opposite sides of the spiral mark the winter solstice.

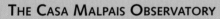

THE CASA MALPAIS OBSERVATORY

Casa Malpais is a Mogollon site in Arizona that contains an astronomical **observatory**. As at Chaco Canyon and Shaw Butte, the sun shines on specific parts of the building during the equinoxes and solstices. Although archaeologists have not found evidence of a link between the site and modern-day Indians, both the Hopi and Zuni consider Casa Malpais **sacred** and believe that their ancestors were part of the Mogollon **culture** that built the site.

large spiral petroglyph halfway between the center of the spiral and the outside. This represents the way the actual equinox divides the time between solstices in half.

The Shaw Butte ruin in Phoenix, Arizona, is believed to contain a Hohokam observatory. The observatory is an oval compound built of **masonry** walls. A large, upright boulder near the compound's center contains petroglyphs consisting of notches and dots. Their positions mark the summer solstice sunset and the winter solstice sunrise. Other stones, markings, and even rooms in the compound align with the sun during the solstices and equinoxes. Archaeologists believe a small rock shelter outside the compound may have been built to act as a calendar. At different times of the year, the sun creates a variety of light patterns on the floor, ledge, and walls of the shelter. These patterns seem to mark the passage of the seasons.

PREHISTORIC FASHION

It is difficult for **archaeologists** to know what types of clothing ancient Indians wore. Fabrics and animal skins break down and disappear fairly quickly. Luckily, some **artifacts** remain, including pieces of sandals and clothing, as well as bits of cordage. From studying these, scientists have pieced together strong theories.

Ancient Clothing

The ancient Indians found many uses for the resources around them. They made sandals and belts from plant fibers and turned cotton, yucca, and agave (*uh GAH vee* or *uh GAY vee*) leaves into cords and yarn.

To make yarn from yucca and agave, the Indians used a thin stone blade to cut the leaves. They then used a rock scraper to separate the flesh and fibers from the leaves. Bunches of fiber were twisted to create long strings that could be woven into fabric on a **loom** or braided or sewn together. Ancestral Puebloans also used human hair to make cords and nets, as did their descendants, the Pueblo. Based on what scientists know about the Pueblo, they believe that only women's hair was used for Ancestral Puebloan cordage. Like the Pueblo, the ancient women wore their hair short—only about 2 inches (5 centimeters) long—so they could keep cutting it as it grew to use in cordage. Men, on the other hand, kept their hair long.

Animal skins, fur, and feathers were also used to make clothing and blankets. To make their famous turkey blankets, Ancestral Puebloans would twist animal fur between pieces

▲ A cotton shirt that scientists believe was woven by an Ancestral Puebloan sometime between A.D. 700 and 1200. To make a cotton garment, ancient people had to extract fibers of cotton from the plant; spin the fibers, by hand, into yarn or thread; and then weave the yarn or thread into fabric. At least some of the weaving was done by men in Ancestral Puebloan society.

of **yucca cordage** to make string. Turkey feathers were then intertwined with the string to make blankets. Desert people did not wear much more than loincloths in the summer, and they wore sandals year-round. In winter, they added shirts made from deer hides, as well as cotton **ponchos**. A poncho is a piece of cloth with a slit in the middle. It is pulled over the head and worn as a cloak.

A Touch of Beauty

Ancient Indians used vegetable dyes to give color to their fabrics. They decorated their clothes with turkey feathers, bits of fur, and shells, bone, or stones. Scientists believe that they probably also wore jewelry daily. Rings and other ornaments were carved from shells, broken pieces of pottery, and animal bones. For necklaces, the artists strung these materials, as well as such semiprecious stones as turquoise, onto strings.

Some prehistoric Indians also seem to have decorated their bodies. Archaeologists have found many paint boxes among Hohokam ruins. These artifacts suggest that the Hohokam painted their faces and bodies, perhaps for ceremonies.

THE SHAPE OF THINGS

Ancestral Puebloans apparently molded their babies' heads. Basketmakers, the early Ancestral Puebloans, used soft, padded cradleboards to carry their children. Sometime around A.D. 700, they removed the padding. The pressure of the plain board on the babies' soft skulls caused them to become flattened in the back.

▲ Pendants, or hanging pieces of jewelry, depict a deer (above top) and a bird (above). Carved from abalone shell with turquoise beads inset for eyes, they were made in about A.D. 1200 by the desert-dwelling Sinagua Indians. The shell must have been obtained through trade with Pacific Coast Indians.

EARLY FARMERS

After corn was introduced to the people of the Southwest about 4,000 years ago, farming became their way of life. The ways in which these groups grew their crops depended on where they lived.

Fruits of the Fields

Corn, squash, and beans were the main crops grown by the Ancestral Puebloans, Mogollon, Hohokam, and Patayan. The Hohokam also grew cotton. To spin cotton into yarn, the Hohokam used a spindle—a long stick with a wheel called a whorl on the bottom. To begin, a woman wetted the end of the raw cotton and stuck it to the spindle down by the whorl. She would rotate the spindle while she used her other hand to pull the cotton into a string. A form of tobacco, probably smoked during ceremonies, was also grown by some groups.

Ancestral Puebloans also **domesticated** and raised turkeys. Experts know this because the remains of turkeys have been found among Ancestral Puebloan ruins. There is little evidence that the birds

TIME TESTED

In *Pueblo Grande Museum Profiles*, Jerry B. Howard, the curator of Anthropology at the **Mesa** Southwest Museum, wrote: "The prehistoric Hohokam constructed one of the largest and most sophisticated irrigation networks ever created using preindustrial technology." Modern engineers used the ancient canals as models when they built an irrigation system in the Salt River Valley in Phoenix. In fact, the earliest modern canals in the area were created simply by cleaning out the Hohokam's canals and adding new sluices (gates to regulate water flow).

▼ The Hohokam used the Salt River to feed their many irrigation canals. The extensive canal system they built allowed the Hohokam to successfully grow crops in an extremely dry region. Some individual canals measured up to 20 miles (32 kilometers) long, and the whole system eventually included hundreds of miles of canals.

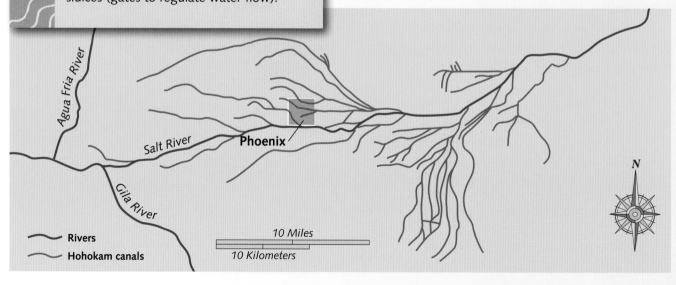

Agua Fria River

Salt River

Phoenix

Gila River

— Rivers
— Hohokam canals

10 Miles
10 Kilometers

N

or their eggs were eaten, though. Instead, **archaeologists** believe that the turkeys were raised for their feathers. They may also have been let loose in gardens to eat crop-damaging bugs.

Life-Giving Water

Early Basketmakers (500 B.C.-A.D. 800) of the Ancestral Puebloan **culture** probably grew their crops in small garden plots. They used a method called dry farming, which relied solely on the region's scant rain. During the Pueblo phase (800-1300), the Ancestral Puebloans developed a system to catch and store rainwater. This allowed them to plant larger plots.

The Patayan planted their crops on the banks of the Colorado River. They and the Early Mogollon (200-1150) counted on rain and the annual flooding of the river to enrich their fields as well as rain to water their crops. By the time

▲ A canal built by the Hohokam to irrigate their crops. Unlike the Mogollon, whose irrigation systems relied on catching and dispersing water, the Hohokam redirected river water through an extensive system of lined ditches.

they reached their Pueblo phase (1150-1400), though, the Mogollon used **irrigation** ditches to water larger and larger fields. While the Mogollon irrigation system relied mainly on rainwater, the system built by the Hohokam actually redirected water from rivers. This much more complicated system used dams made of logs, brush, and woven mats to channel water from rivers into irrigation canals. Hohokam engineers controlled the water flow by gently sloping the bottoms of the channels. One way they reduced water loss from the canals was by plastering the bottoms of the ditches. Over the years, the Hohokam built a vast network that eventually included more than 600 miles (965 kilometers) of canals.

THE LAND PROVIDES

Although the farming techniques used by ancient Indians improved over time, they continued to rely on hunting and gathering to supplement their diets and to provide food when their crops failed.

▲ Many varieties of cactus provided food for the Indians of the Southwest. The Hohokam used long sticks to knock fruit from the arms of the tall saguaro cactus. Prickly pear fruit could be harvested by hand. Some scientists believe that in addition to foraging for desert plants, the Hohokam transplanted cholla and prickly pear plants along the outside borders of their crops.

Hunting for a Meal

Ancient Indians most likely ate small animals more often than large game. Scientists believe the Ancestral Puebloans probably used nets to trap mice and rabbits. The largest hunting net yet discovered was found at White Dog Cave in Arizona. It measures 240 feet (73 meters) long and almost 4 feet (1.2 meters) wide and weighs 28 pounds (13 kilograms). **Archaeologists** believe that the net was probably used to capture a large group of small animals at once. Archaeologists speculate that Mogollon hunters may

BISON HUNTERS

Bison are usually considered animals of the Great Plains, not the desert. However, archaeologists have found evidence that some Mogollon bands hunted bison. One prehistoric site discovered in Mogollon territory was littered with bison bones.

have trapped beavers along streams and wild turkeys that lived in the mountains. People who lived by rivers, such as the Hohokam and Patayan, most likely also used nets to catch fish. The Hohokam hunted small animals, such as lizards and snakes, as well as larger game, such as mountain sheep and antelope.

Before A.D. 400, early Mogollon, Hohokam, and Basketmaker hunters used spears and a special spear-throwing device called an **atlatl** *(AHT lah tuhl)* to hunt big game. After about 400, however, the Mogollon and Hohokam used the bow and arrow to hunt. Later Basketmakers eventually adopted the bow and arrow from their Mogollon neighbors.

Gathering Nature's Bounty

The desert can be an excellent source of wild plants—if one knows where to look. For the ancient Indians of the Southwest, being able to identify a variety of edible plants was crucial to their survival.

Ancestral Puebloan women gathered a grain called amaranth, piñon *(PIHN yuhn* or *PEEN yohn)* nuts from pine trees, sunflower seeds, and Indian rice grass to supplement their crops. The Hohokam gathered mesquite *(mehs KEET)* beans from the trees that grew along the riverbank and gathered the fruits of saguaro *(suh GWAH roh* or *suh WAH roh)*, cholla *(CHOY uh)*, prickly pear, and barrel cactus. They also collected acorns and berries in the mountains.

Like the Hohokam, the Mogollon visited the mountains to gather wild fruits and seeds. They also harvested the fruit of desert plants, including mesquite, yucca, agave, and prickly pear cactus.

▼ The **petroglyphs** at Newspaper Rock in Utah are at least 1,500 years old and cover 200 square feet (18.5 square meters) of a cliff wall. They include images of people and animals, including some of the larger game hunted by ancient Indians of the Southwest.

FOOD FOR TODAY AND TOMORROW

Farming improved the diet of ancient people. It also gave them extra food to store for winter or lean times. Over time, ancient Indians developed better ways to prepare and store food. **Artifacts** reveal how.

Feeding the Family

Ancient Indians skinned such small animals as squirrels and lizards and ate them raw or roasted them whole over a fire. They skinned and gutted larger animals where they were killed. Once home, the Indians cut the meat into smaller pieces for roasting or stewing or sliced it into strips and dried it in the sun.

Preparing grains and other food from plants took more effort. The ancient Indians had to soak beans before cooking them and remove the shells from nuts and seeds. Corn was cooked in a pottery jar by the fire or ground into flour. Prehistoric women used **manos** *(MAH nohz)* and **metates** to grind corn, nuts, and seeds into fine flour for cooking. A mano is a hand stone used to crush grains in the metate. Grinding was hard work that took hours.

Early Basketmakers used watertight baskets for cooking. Instead of placing the

◄ Ears of dried corn discovered by archaeologists excavating a storage pit at the Gila Cliff Dwellings in New Mexico. Although the corn had been there for hundreds of years after the Mogollon left the site, the kernels were perfectly preserved thanks to the region's hot, dry climate.

basket over a fire, they dropped hot stones into the food
mixture. In later years, sometime around A.D. 800, they began
using cooking pots placed directly over the fire.
The Patayan also used stone-lined pits to roast large
pieces of meat.

Food for Lean Times

Stored foods, such as flour, dried meat, vegetables, and fruit,
helped ancient people survive when fresh food was scarce.
They often dried corn right on the cob. They thinly sliced
other vegetables, such as squash, and dried them.

Early Basketmakers (500 B.C.-A.D. 800) used baskets for
storage. The Patayan used sealed pottery jars. The early
Mogollon (A.D. 200-600) stored their extra food in small pits
and, later, in large pots. Late in their history (A.D. 1150-
1400), the Mogollon and other groups built stone rooms
specifically for food storage.

▲ Corn-grinding bins discovered at the Betatakin *(but TAT uh kihn)* Cliff Dwellings on
the Shonto Plateau overlooking the Tsegi
Canyon in Arizona. Ancient Puebloan women
must have worked side-by-side grinding the
corn at this three-station bin. The flat, slanted
stones were used as the grinding surfaces.
Small handheld stones like the one shown
in the bin on the right were used as manos.

TOUGH ON THE TEETH

The teeth of ancient Indians
show a lot of wear. **Archaeologists** speculate that their
teeth wore down because
small pieces of stone metates
and manos, used to grind
grains, often ended up in
the food.

LIFE LESSONS

In ancient Indian **cultures**, children learned by example. Girls watched their mothers and aunts as they went about their daily chores. Boys copied the ways of their fathers and uncles.

Learning the Ways of the People

Archaeologists believe that children became adults in Mogollon society between the ages of 9 and 15 years old. The remains of young Mogollon children are not usually found buried with tools or weapons. More adult items, such as tools and ceremonial items, are usually found with the remains of people judged to be age 9 and older.

▲ Three generations of women grind corn using stone metates and **manos**, the same method used by the Ancestral Puebloans, Mogollon, Hohokam, and Patayan to make corn meal. Girls learned such skills by watching their mothers and grandmothers.

A HARD, SHORT LIFE
Archaeologists believe that as many as half of Mogollon children died before the age of 12. By studying the skeletons found at Mogollon sites, scientists can tell that most of the children died from poor nutrition or diseases that are considered treatable today.

In societies that have no written language, storytelling is often used to teach children about the ways of their people. Archaeologists assume that village elders taught children history and folkways by telling them stories of how their people were created or how they first received the gift of corn.

From the time they were in cradleboards, children accompanied their mothers as they gathered wild foods and tended their crops. They probably began picking berries and gathering nuts not long after they took their first steps.

Little girls probably worked alongside their mothers at the **metates** from the time they were very young. They might have learned to make baskets and pottery by first watching their mothers and then experimenting themselves. Boys probably learned to trap and hunt animals from the time they could walk behind the older men. In preparation for his ceremonial role in the community, a young man would probably have spent a lot of time in a **kiva**. In **matrilineal** societies, such as the Ancestral Puebloans, the boy would have had his lessons in the kiva belonging to his mother's family. His uncles, rather than his father, would have taught him.

◀ Baskets were very important to Ancestral Puebloans of the Basketmaker period. They were used for everything from gathering, to storage, to cooking. Girls would have learned how to weave these beautiful baskets—and create intricate designs—by watching the older women in the village.

THE LIGHTER SIDE OF LIFE

For people living in ancient societies, the simple act of survival required a great deal of time and effort. Scientists believe that, despite this, people still managed to find time for entertainment.

Toys and Games

Archaeologists have found what might be toys at many ancient Indian sites. Examples include tiny dolls and miniature animal carvings made by the Hohokam and miniature pots created by the Ancestral Puebloans. It is difficult for scientists to determine whether these items were really toys or if they were ceremonial objects. A small carving of an antelope, for example, could have been created to bring good luck to a hunter.

▼ An intact Ancient Puebloan ball court at Wupatki *(wu PAT kee)* **Pueblo** in Arizona. Archaeologists believe that spectators sat on the low, rounded walls, which had entryways on both ends. Scientists have no exact knowledge of how the game was played but are fairly certain that its function was both ceremonial and for entertainment.

MESOAMERICAN ROOTS

Many Mesoamerican peoples, including the Aztec and Maya, played a ball game on courts similar to those found in Hohokam settlements. Scientists believe that the Hohokam adopted this game from their neighbors to the south.

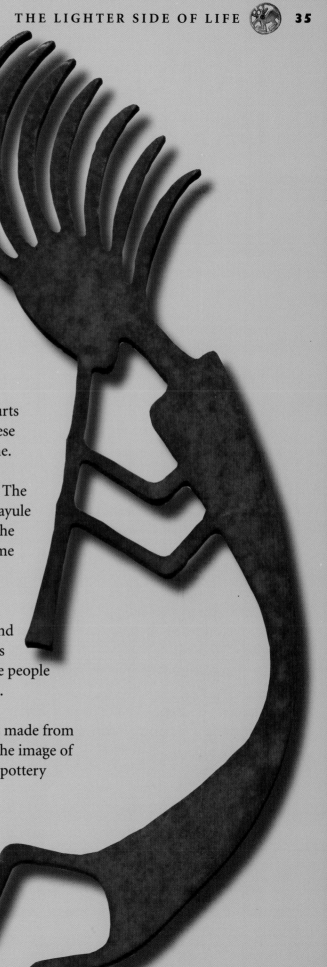

Archaeologists have also found gaming pieces among Ancestral Puebloan ruins. These pieces include shaped stones and bones. Scientists believe that the Ancestral Puebloans, like their descendants, probably used these pieces to gamble. Scientists also believe that the Ancestral Puebloans enjoyed such sporting events as footraces.

The Hohokam first built ball courts around A.D. 500. The courts were oval structures made of dirt with low rounded walls. These walls were probably used as seats for people watching the game. The courts, which had no roofs, had entryways on either end. They usually had stone markers at each end and in the center. The players used balls made from a rubberlike substance called guayule (*gwah YOO lay*). Archaeologists have no real idea about how the game was played. They are fairly certain, however, that the game had a ceremonial purpose as well as providing entertainment.

Music and Dancing

Musical instruments have been found among ancient ruins, and **petroglyphs** often feature dancers and musicians. Instruments were most likely developed for ceremonies and **rituals**, but the people probably also enjoyed listening to music at other times as well.

Excavations at Basketmaker sites have unearthed flutes, rattles made from deer hooves and bones, and whistles made from bird bones. The image of Kokopelli—a flute-playing god—first appeared on Hohokam pottery sometime after A.D. 750.

▶ The image of Kokopelli is closely associated with the Indians of the Southwest. The deity is usually shown playing a flute, which suggests that music was an important part of the ancient Indians' daily lives. Musical instruments are among the artifacts found at the sites of ancient Indian settlements.

HOUSES IN THE EARTH

During the time that they still relied heavily on hunting and gathering, ancient Indians of the Southwest lived in rock overhangs or caves. Later, as they began growing crops and became more settled, they lived in **pit houses**.

Digging for a Home

To build a pit house, the people first had to dig a hole in the ground. They then built a shelter over the pit. The shelter was made of wooden posts that were covered with brush or bundles of reeds. These were smeared with mud or clay. This type of construction is called **wattle and daub**. A spot was left open in the wall for an entrance; a hole in the roof allowed smoke from the fire to escape. Pit houses could be circular, oval, rectangular, or D-shaped.

Many pit houses had a fire pit and storage pits dug into the floor. People slept either on mats on the floor or on low platforms. They kept their personal items on the floor or a platform or hung them from walls.

Early Settlements

Hohokam pit houses were built in groups around a courtyard. Each group consisted of the dwellings of an extended family. Villages were made up of a number of courtyard groups. In later years, around A.D. 975, the Hohokam built larger villages. Each village had one large central courtyard instead of several small courtyards.

▲ Step House at **Mesa** Verde National Park in Colorado contains the ruins of Basket-maker pit houses. Experts believe the dwellings were built and occupied around A.D. 626. The Ancestral Puebloans settled in this same spot again, around A.D. 1226, and built a **pueblo**.

Basketmaker and Mogollon villages were similar. One family occupied a pit house and shared a larger storage pit house with a related family. The families also shared open-sided shelters called **ramadas**. Ramadas offered an outdoor workspace that was shielded from the sun.

The Patayan probably had large base camps that housed a number of families. Scientists speculate that from the base camps, families moved into smaller, temporary villages. Each village, called a **rancheria** (RAN chuh REE uh), was set up for a specific purpose. A rancheria might be located near crops or close to a quarry where stone tools could be crafted, for example.

In all cases, people probably slept or worked inside only during wet or cold weather. Villages included common areas outside where the people spent most of their time.

INFORMATION FROM GARBAGE

Most villages contained **middens**, or garbage dumps. These sites, which often contain bits of pottery, tools, and animal bones, provide **archaeologists** with important clues about the lives of the people who used them. For example, the animal bones tell scientists what kind of foods the people ate.

▼ A model of what a Basketmaker village may have looked like during the period from about A.D. 500 to 700. Archaeologists make such models based on the **artifacts** they find at ancient sites, including the remains of houses, fire pits, and tools.

VILLAGES OF STONE

Around A.D. 700-800, the Mogollon and Ancestral Puebloans stopped living in **pit houses** and began building above-ground structures. Later visitors to the area named these buildings **pueblos** (*pueblo* is a Spanish word that means *town*).

The First Pueblos

The earliest pueblos had walls made of sticks covered with clay. The sticks were anchored to a row of foundation stones. These pueblos were usually large enough for only one family.

Later, above-ground dwellings were made of stones that were held together with mud or clay. The ancient Indians began building dwellings for more than one family around A.D. 900-1000. These complexes resemble modern Puebloan structures, such as the Taos Pueblo in New

▲ A cliff dwelling at Keet Seel, which is now part of Navajo National Monument in Arizona. Ancestral Puebloans lived at the site for a relatively short period in the late 1200's.

Mexico. The Indians often plastered the interior walls and covered them with painted designs. When people stopped living in pit houses, they found new uses for the pits. As before, the holes in the ground were used for storage. These holes were bigger than ordinary storage areas, though, and were probably shared by several people. The people might have also used these areas as meeting places—the first **kivas**. When the people started living in pueblos, religious societies began using kivas to hold meetings and ceremonies. The larger Great Kivas—like modern kivas—were probably used only for religious purposes, not merely for meetings.

At Hovenweep, on the border of Colorado and southeastern Utah, **archaeologists** discovered a settlement built by Ancestral Puebloans. Like other pueblos, the rooms and kivas at Hovenweep were built of shaped sandstone blocks. Hovenweep differs from other pueblos, though. The site does not contain a Great Kiva. Instead, the people of Hovenweep built ceremonial towers.

Cities in the Cliffs

Around A.D. 1150, Ancestral Puebloans began building their famous cliff dwellings. These were entire cities built into the side of a cliff. Most cliff dwellings were built on south-facing ledges. The villages received sunlight even in the winter, and the overhanging lip of the cliff offered shade in the summer.

Some archaeologists believe Ancestral Puebloans built their homes into cliffs to free up valuable land on the **mesa** above for farming. Others suggest that the ancient people built cliff dwellings as protection from invaders. These villages could be reached only by small handholds and toeholds chiseled into the steep canyon walls and were, therefore, difficult to enter.

MYSTERIOUS ENTRIES

The doorways in the above-ground structures of Southwest Indians are often T-shaped. Some archaeologists speculate that this shape made it easier for a person carrying something on his or her shoulders to pass through. Others think the shape made it easier to keep cold air out. People might have draped a blanket over the ledge formed by the upper part of the T so that it hung over the bottom part of the door. This might have kept the worst of the wind out. Smoke from an interior fire could have escaped through the upper part of the T door. Other archaeologists speculate that the shape may have had spiritual significance.

CHACO CANYON: THE CENTER OF THEIR WORLD

The settlement at Chaco Canyon, New Mexico, was a major center of Ancestral Puebloan **culture**. A far-reaching roadway system connected multistory buildings called great houses in Chaco to more than 150 buildings throughout the region.

A Planned City

The Chaco settlement was built over a period from about A.D. 850 to 1150. The great houses found there had hundreds of rooms and were bigger than anything the Puebloans had built before. In fact, one of the houses, **Pueblo Bonito**, was the biggest multifamily residence on Earth—and would remain so for 700 years. With at least 600 rooms and 40 **kivas**, it was, in essence, the largest apartment building in the world until a larger complex was constructed in New York City in 1887! The great houses at Chaco were often positioned using cardinal directions; that is, according to positions as they

▼ The Chaco settlement is made up of several great houses and their kivas. The great houses include Una Vida (150 rooms and 5 kivas); Pueblo Bonito (600 rooms and 40 kivas); Chetro Kelt (500 rooms and 16 kivas); Pueblo del Arroyo (280 rooms and more than 20 kivas); and Kin Kletso (100 rooms and 5 kivas). The largest known Great Kiva in the Chaco settlement is called Casa Ricondada.

appear on the compass—north, south, east, and west. The ancient builders accomplished this without the benefit of an actual compass. They determined directions by studying the position of the sun over the course of the year.

More than 400 miles (650 kilometers) of roads connected the great houses at Chaco to others throughout the region. The roads were not simply foot trails that were worn into roads over the years. From 8 to 10 feet (2.5 to 3 meters) wide, these Chacoan roads were built by digging down to sandstone bedrock.

Shrouded in Mystery

Archaeologists are not sure what purpose Chaco served. Some believe that such a large, spread-out settlement guaranteed that everyone had enough food. If a crop failed in one area, for example, people from another area could share their crops with others in the settlement. Others think Chaco was a trading center. It is also possible that Chaco was a spiritual center, where ancient people came to share ceremonies.

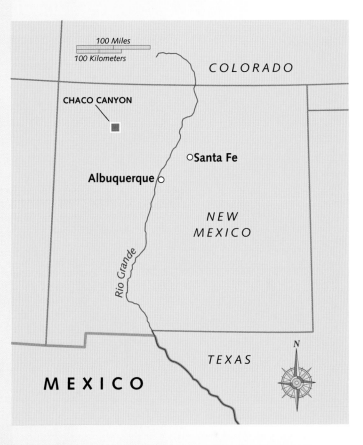

▲ The Chaco Canyon settlement is located in the northwest corner of present-day New Mexico. Many Indians of the area trace the roots of their **clans** back to this site. Several Pueblo groups, including the Acoma and Zuni, have stories that tell of certain clans migrating from Chaco to their present-day locations in New Mexico. Ten different Hopi clans also trace their ancestry to the site.

STAYING IN TOUCH

The people in the Chaco great houses used hilltop signaling stations to communicate with other settlements. Archaeologists working in the area have found the remains of signal fires, as well as **obsidian** slabs. Obsidian is a dark natural glass that is formed when **magma** (molten rock) cools. Prehistoric people used polished pieces of obsidian as mirrors, which could be used to reflect sunlight to create a signal.

Chaco Canyon contained many Great Kivas, which were typically from 40 to 70 feet (12 to 20 meters) in diameter and from 12 to 16 feet (4 to 5 meters) deep.

From the mid-1100's into the 1200's, construction slowed at Chaco, and its role as the center of Ancestral Puebloan life ended. People moved to other areas and created new settlements. Why the people abandoned Chaco is one of the great mysteries surrounding the settlement.

SIGNS OF TROUBLE?

The archaeological record of warfare among ancient Indians of the Southwest is confusing. Although researchers have not found a lot of evidence of violence, many villages were built like fortresses.

Built for Defense

The Early Pit House Mogollon (A.D. 200-600) built their first villages on high land that could be easily defended. At the very least, their position would help the villagers spot approaching enemies. They also sometimes built walls around their communities. **Archaeologists** have found no solid evidence of violence among the ruins of these villages, however.

The Late Pit House Mogollon (600-1150) may have felt more secure because they started building their villages in easier-to-reach areas closer to their fields. They also seem to have stopped building walls around their villages. The Mogollon were also one of the first people to adopt the bow and arrow. Some archaeologists suggest that having this weapon made them less worried about possible enemies.

▶ Montezuma Castle in Arizona is one of the best-preserved cliff dwellings in North America. It must have also been one of the best protected; staging an attack on it would have been difficult if not impossible. The buildings are surrounded on three sides by sheer cliff walls, and there are no door or window openings on the lower levels.

▲ Ancestral Puebloan arrows found at Chaco Canyon in New Mexico. The wooden shafts have stone points attached. The Ancestral Puebloans also used feathers to steady an arrow's flight.

The famous cliff dwellings of the Ancestral Puebloans also appear to have been constructed for defense. Because the lodgings are built directly into the side of a cliff, no one could attack from the rear. The villages were also difficult to reach from the front. The courtyards could be reached only by shallow toeholds and handholds chipped into the face of the rock or by ladders that could quickly be pulled up in times of attack. However, as with the Mogollon, there are relatively few signs of violence among the many ruins of the Ancestral Puebloans.

The Peaceful Ones

Long after their neighbors moved on to stone structures, the Hohokam continued to build **wattle and daub** dwellings. Their villages were not surrounded by walls or other protective barriers. The Hohokam lived in Snaketown continuously for more than 1,000 years. Archaeologists have found no trace of violence or warfare among the ruins of that site. These facts suggest that these were a peaceful people and that they were not troubled by outside enemies.

UNCLEAR EVIDENCE

Although archaeologists have found evidence of violence and conflict among the Ancestral Puebloans and other Southwestern groups, interpreting the evidence can be difficult. It can sometimes be hard to determine whether a person was killed by violence or by accident. For example, a smashed skull could be the result of a fall or a deliberate blow to the head. Even though some remains show evidence of wounds that seem to indicate warfare, lack of written accounts makes understanding the circumstances of death difficult.

TIME FOR BEAUTY

Over time, the people of the Southwest developed better ways to prepare and store food. These advances gave the people more free time. Many used this time to make beautiful everyday objects or works of art.

Stone Art

The Hohokam probably had more free time than any of the other ancient **cultures** of the Southwest. Thanks to their **irrigation** canals, they were able to spend less time taking care of their crops. **Archaeologists** believe that they used this free time to create works of art.

Ancient people had long used stone to make tools, including knives, scrapers, hammers, and arrowheads. In the late A.D. 700's, the Hohokam came up with new uses for stone. They carved bowls from stone in the shapes of birds, reptiles, and other animals. They made other stone and ceramic vessels, such as censers that were used to burn incense, in the shapes of animals and human beings. A container that is made in the shape of an animal or person is called an effigy (*EF a gee*) vessel. The Hohokam made many ceramic effigy vessels.

▼ A stone mortar in the shape of a horned toad, dating from around A.D. 900, was found at the Hohokam settlement called Snaketown in present-day Arizona. Experts believe the vessel was used to grind pigments to make paint.

The Hohokam also began making realistic ceramic figurines around this time. They decorated the pieces with black or red painted "tattoos" and bits of clay to represent clothing. Hohokam **artisans** later made hand-molded ceramic heads that were probably attached to cloth bodies to make dolls. Experts are not sure whether these dolls were meant as toys or had ceremonial functions.

Etchings in Shell

Sometime after A.D. 900, the Hohokam discovered the art of etching, which they used to make shell **ornaments**. To create these unique decorations, the artists drew a design on a shell using pitch (resin from a pine tree). They then dipped the shell into a jar of acid that may have been made from the juice of saguaro cactus fruit. The acid ate away the exposed part of the shell, leaving the pitch-covered design behind. The shells were then sometimes painted.

Archaeologists believe that families or even entire communities probably specialized in certain crafts. A discovery at Shelltown near Tucson, Arizona— which included shell dust, unfinished ornaments, and other waste products— supports this theory. The remains indicate that a whole community of artisans lived and worked here producing shell products.

> **PIONEERING AN ART FORM**
> The Hohokam perfected the art of etching hundreds of years before Europeans developed a similar technique to etch designs onto helmets, shields, and body armor. Instead of using pitch to coat the metal, Europeans used wax to cover the entire piece. The artist then scraped a design into the wax and dipped the piece in acid.

▶ An etched shell ornament—a specialty craft of the Hohokam—found in the Tucson Mountains in Arizona. The desert-dwelling Hohokam acquired the shells through trade with other Indian groups.

ROCK ART

The Indians of the Southwest developed several forms of rock art. This art includes painted images called **pictograms** *(PIHK tuh gramz)* and chiseled images called **petroglyphs**. Tens of thousands of these mysterious works can be found on rocks, boulders, and cliffs throughout the Southwest. Some groups also made **geoglyphs** *(JEE uh glihfz)*, enormous etchings depicting animals and people, on the desert floor. Geoglyphs are also sometimes called **intaglios** *(ihn TAL yohz* or *ihn TAHL yohz)*.

Symbols in Stone

Many of the symbols found in rock art are similar to those found on a particular **culture's** pottery. Those, and the location of the art, are two clues that help **archaeologists** figure out which group created it. Unfortunately, those facts do not explain what the pictures mean. Even an image of something as simple as a hunter spearing an antelope cannot be taken at face value. Perhaps it records a hunt. Or it might have been made as part of a ceremony to ensure a successful hunt.

Some symbols are connected to certain **clans** and may have been used to mark territory. Other symbols seem to have a religious meaning. They may represent legends and might have been used in a **ritual**. Still other symbols seem to represent the sun, moon, and stars and could have been used to track the passing of the seasons.

Unlocking the Mystery

Archaeologists also have trouble dating these ancient works of art. Scientists often rely on a process called **radiocarbon dating** to determine the age of certain **artifacts**. All living things

◀ A petroglyph at Newspaper Rock in Utah. Experts sometimes struggle to understand the meaning of such images. Although petroglyphs of animals seem obvious enough, it is hard to guess what the large central picture represents.

PATAYAN DESERT ART

The most famous examples of Patayan art are the intaglios (art consisting of figures or designs sunk below the surface) found near Blythe, California. First, the artists scraped away a thin layer of dark soil to expose a lighter layer of soil below. Then, they shaped the scrapings into the images of giant human figures, geometric shapes, and animals. The largest of the intaglios is almost 300 feet (90 meters) long and can only be viewed from above, leading archaeologists to assume they were meant as messages to their ancestors or to the spirit world.

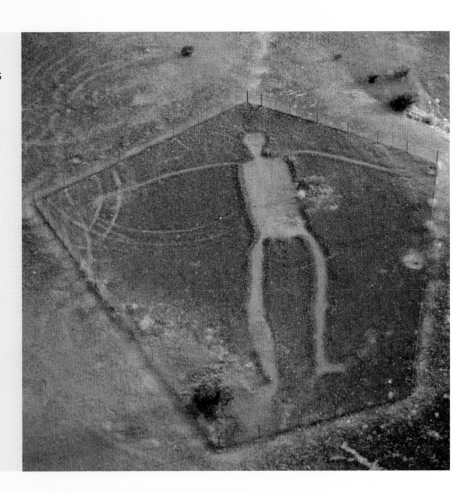

contain radiocarbon, a type of carbon that plants absorb from the air and that people and animals take in by eating plants. After a living thing dies, the radiocarbon breaks down at a set rate. By measuring how much radiocarbon remains in an object, scientists can determine when the living thing died. Unfortunately, because rock is not a living thing, radiocarbon dating does not help scientists determine a date for a piece of rock art.

Sometimes scientists date petroglyphs based on their content. For example, a petroglyph in Canyon De Chelly in Arizona shows people on horseback. Because Spanish people introduced horses to the area, archaeologists know that the petroglyph must have been created after the arrival of the Spaniards. Another way to date a petroglyph is to determine the age of the **desert varnish** on the surface of the rock. Desert varnish is the glossy coating of certain chemicals found on rocks and pebbles after long exposure in desert regions.

EVERYDAY WORKS OF ART

The ancient people of the Southwest used pots and baskets for everyday tasks. However, the beauty of these objects qualifies them as works of art.

Beautiful Baskets

The Ancestral Puebloans made a variety of baskets from braided or tightly coiled plant fibers. They created designs with dye or by varying the type of fiber or weaving pattern.

The Basketmakers made a variety of carrying baskets, including some that were worn over the shoulders like a backpack. Some baskets, used for storing water and cooking, were tightly woven and lined with pitch to make them watertight. Other baskets were used to store food. When **archaeologists** found some of these baskets hundreds of years after they were made, the food inside was still protected.

The Ancestral Puebloans gradually adopted pottery for cooking, storage, and ceremonial uses starting around A.D. 600. By this time, other ancient peoples of the Southwest had been making pottery for hundreds of years. As the Ancestral Puebloans turned their skills to making pots, the craft of basketmaking declined.

Priceless Pots

Pottery can tell archaeologists where a certain group lived and when they lived there. Changes in pottery can also show how a **culture** changed over time.

▶ A Mogollon jar dating from approximately A.D. 1025-1150. The **artisan** who created the jar covered it with a white slip before using red paint to add geometric patterns.

Techniques for making pottery came to Southwest Indians from older cultures in Mexico. To make pots, early peoples gathered clay, ground it up, and then mixed it with water to form a paste. They then rolled the clay into long coils, which were used to build the pot. After they added each coil, they smoothed the pot and squeezed the coils together.

They often rubbed the pot with a smooth stone before firing (heating) it. They also covered many vessels with a **slip**, or thin layer of wet, fine clay. The slip was often white and probably made the vessel easier to decorate.

Early Indians decorated the pottery in several ways. Sometimes they pinched the clay coils to make patterns. Some groups pressed plants into the sides of the wet pot to create designs. They also decorated pots with paints made from vegetables and fruits.

A SENSE OF STYLE
Each culture had a pottery style associated with each stage of its development. Early pots were typically plain gray or brown. Around A.D. 300, the Mogollon and Hohokam started making decorated pottery. The Ancestral Puebloans followed, beginning around A.D. 600.

▶ A black and white bowl featuring the image of a bat was made by the Mimbres, a small band of Mogollon who remain famous for their black-on-white pottery. Mimbres pottery designs are usually classified as either naturalistic, featuring people or animals; or abstract, which were more difficult to interpret. Most other ancient groups created abstract designs.

GREAT CULTURES IN DECLINE

By the end of the 1400's, the ancient settlements in the Southwest had been abandoned. Some declined slowly. In other cases, researchers believe that entire villages emptied all at once.

From Boom to Bust

Around A.D. 1250, a group of Ancestral Puebloans lived in a cliff dwelling called Betatakin *(buh TAT uh kihn)*, meaning *ledge house* in Navajo, at Tsegi *(SAY yee)* Canyon in Arizona. For several years, they gathered enough material to build a new village nearby. In 1275, an entire community moved there. They continued building for 11 more years—but then suddenly abandoned the settlement.

Major construction was also going on at Keet Seel (*potsherd* in Navajo), another Tsegi Canyon site during the 1270's. Then, just as at Betatakin, the people at Keet Seel stopped building in the mid-1280's. **Archaeologists** believe that, unlike at Betatakin, the people of Keet Seel abandoned the village one or two families at a time.

Societies on the Move

Many Mogollon sites in Arizona were deserted around the same time as those in Tsegi Canyon. **Archaeologists** believe that what happened at Grasshopper Ruin might have happened in other areas. By the mid-1300's, the population at Grasshopper was so large that the people had probably used up all of the available natural resources. They had cut down many trees for use in building their dwellings, and all the farmland in the immediate area was being used. Over time, the Mogollon began moving north, where many seem to have joined Ancestral Puebloan villages.

◀ Archaeologists excavate Ancestral Puebloan ruins in Colorado to learn about the **culture** that lived in the area. **Excavating** ancient ruins is done very carefully. Workers uncover only small areas at a time to avoid breaking fragile **artifacts**.

LOST AND FOUND

For a time, archaeologists believed that the people who built the magnificent cliff dwellings and sophisticated irrigation systems in the Southwest simply disappeared. Scientists now know from archaeological evidence that these people were the ancestors of later Indian groups. Pieces of pottery and tools found throughout the area show that the Ancestral Puebloans **migrated** to territories later occupied by the Pueblo. Descendants also shared many of their ancestors' cultural practices, such as methods of farming and craft production.

Others may have abandoned farming and returned to hunting and gathering for food. Still others may have wandered east toward the Great Plains.

Between 1400 and 1450, the Hohokam also abandoned their communities and the sophisticated **irrigation** systems they had built. Some of them might have joined Ancestral Puebloan communities. Many of the people returned to their simpler farming ways of planting small crops close to water sources, such as rivers. Experts know this because the Hohokam did not build new irrigation systems after relocating. These groups are believed to be the ancestors of the Pima and Tohono O'odham. Likewise, it is believed that the Patayan were the ancestors of the people later called the Yuma and Mohave *(moh HAH vee)*.

▼ Such artifacts as Ancestral Puebloan potsherds, bone tools, and dried corncobs allow archaeologists to reconstruct how ancient people lived. Dried corncobs and **manos** present a clear picture of the types of food the people ate and how they prepared them. Even fragments of pottery and tools can offer a lot of information on how ancient people lived and worked.

WHY DID THEY LEAVE?

Ancient Indians of the Southwest apparently left their lands at the peak of their **cultures**. Scientists have long searched for an answer as to why they would simply abandon all they had worked so hard to achieve.

A Long Dry Spell

Scientists once believed that the Indians were driven away by the Great Drought, which lasted from 1276 to 1299. A long dry spell would have made farming difficult and stunted the growth of wild foods.

Usually during times of drought, some families would leave the village to find better fields. This would explain why a settlement would empty out a little at a time. It would not, however, explain the total abandonment of such sites as Betatakin. The ancient Indians had also lived through droughts in the past. Each time they adapted to their

◀ The Arizona desert is a harsh environment. The plants that grow there are few and far between—even during periods of plentiful rain. Surviving in this area presented many challenges to ancient Indian peoples, especially during droughts.

circumstances. They did not abandon their territory entirely. Therefore, **archaeologists** believe there must have been additional reasons for the Indians to leave their land.

Push and Pull

Some archaeologists believe that warfare might have pushed the Indians to leave their homes. **Nomadic** tribes, such as the Apache and Navajo, arrived in the area sometime between A.D. 1100 and 1450. These tribes often attacked other tribes, perhaps raiding their food supplies. Other archaeologists think that violence may have broken out among the four ancient groups. Like a long dry spell, these threats could have helped push the ancient Indians off their traditional lands.

Still other researchers speculate that many ancient peoples might have been drawn to more fertile areas to the south and east where water was more abundant. Perhaps Ancestral Puebloans decided to settle among the people in the Rio Grande area because water was more plentiful there.

▼ **Petroglyphs** located close to the Rio Grande in New Mexico are believed to have been created in the 1200's, providing further evidence of when Ancient Indians **migrated** to the area.

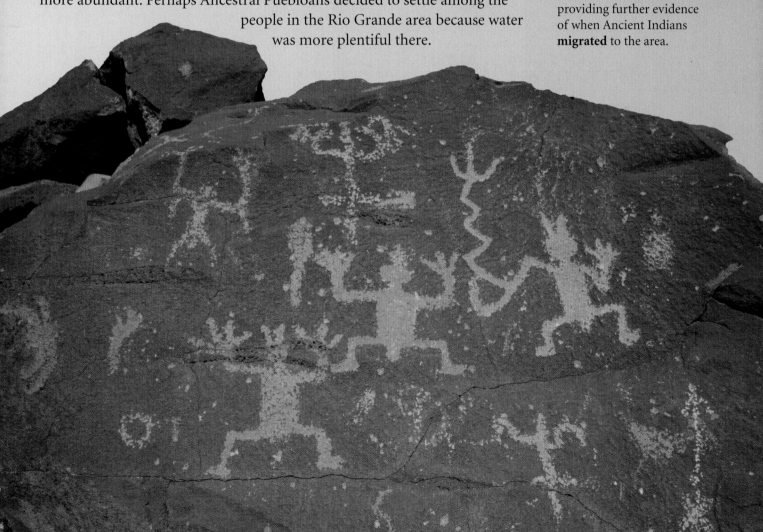

TRACES OF THE VANISHED ONES

During the period of **migration**, some of the Hohokam remained in their original territory but turned back to a much simpler existence. Scientists believe this group gave rise to the Pima and Tohono O'odham Indians.

Traditional Lifestyles

Like the Hohokam, the Tohono O'odham and Pima were **seminomadic** (*SEHM ee noh MAD ihk*) people who lived along the Colorado River. They lived in dome-shaped houses made of wooden poles and covered with brush and dirt. The Tohono O'odham and Pima farmed the land near the river and added to their diets by hunting and gathering wild foods.

The most valuable wild food available to the Tohono O'odham was the fruit of the saguaro cactus. In late June, the women would harvest the red buds of the tall cactus using special poles. Each pole was made out of two saguaro ribs with a hook, made of greasewood branch, on top. The women would use the poles

▲ The Pima round house (or *olas-ki*) was used during cooler weather. The Pima only abandoned this traditional type of dwelling—made from willow, arrowweed, cottonwood, and mud—in the early 1900's.

to knock the ripe fruits off the cacti. They then dried the saguaro fruit pulp and formed it into small cakes. These cakes could be stored for long periods and then boiled in water to be eaten. The juice from the fresh fruit was boiled and made into a fermented liquid, which played an important role in the tribe's rain festivals.

These desert tribes divided their communities into groups called **moieties** *(MOY uh teez)*. The moieties were further divided into smaller groups. In this **patrilineal** society, the children belonged to the group—and therefore the moiety—of their fathers.

Each village had a ceremonial leader called the Keeper of the Smoke and a medicine man who was responsible for the well-being of the community. The Pima medicine man who was responsible for curing sickness was called the Siatcokam.

▼ Tohono O'odham children perform a traditional tribal dance during a celebration at Tumacacori National Monument in Arizona. Passing on tribal customs and traditions is one way Indians keep their heritage alive.

LIFE ON THE RESERVATION

Today, the Tohono O'odham and Pima live on **reservations**—areas of land set aside for Indians by the United States government. Like many Indian groups, the Tohono O'odham and Pima work hard to hold onto their traditions. The Tohono O'odham Basketweavers Association celebrates the culture's heritage by keeping the craft a living art. The Tohono O'odham's native language is also still spoken on the reservation. The Pima keep many of their customs through the Gila River Arts and Crafts Center, which is located on their reservation near Phoenix, Arizona.

The Center coordinates arts and crafts fairs and festivals that feature traditional music and dancing.

DESCENDANTS OF THE OLD PEOPLE

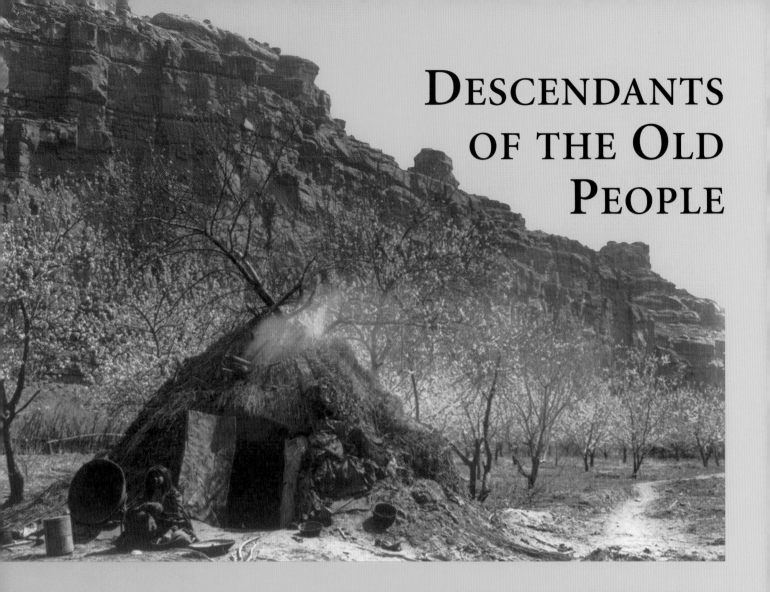

Archaeologists believe the River and Upland Yuma and the Mohave may be descended from the Patayan. These groups occupied the traditional homeland of their ancestors and followed a similar way of life.

River People

The River Yuma and Mohave lived in their ancestors' homeland near the lower Colorado River when the Spanish arrived in 1602. Like the Patayan, these people raised corn, beans, squash, and other crops. They also hunted, fished, and gathered wild plants, especially mesquite beans.

Like other **seminomadic** tribes, the Yuma and Mohave lived in dome-shaped huts made of brush. Their settlements generally consisted of several hundred people. However, the Yuma and Mohave were not as peaceful as their ancestors. They fought over territory and trade routes and also for captives. The Mohave, like other Indian tribes of the time, captured people from other tribes and made them slaves.

▲ A 1903 photo of a Havasupai woman sitting in front of a type of dwelling called a wickiup (*WIHK ee UHP*). The wickiup, made of mud and brush, was usually used during the summer, when the people lived in the bottom of Havasu Canyon and tended their crops. In the winter, the Havasupai Indians would move up to the plateaus, where they lived in rock alcoves or wickiups made of brush.

Upland Groups

Another group of Yuma, known as the Upland Yuma, lived in western Arizona south of the Grand Canyon. Some Upland Yuma tended garden plots near canyon streams in the summer. They also grew corn, beans, and squash. The Upland Yuma relied on hunting such animals as bighorn sheep and gathering wild foods. Yucca, an agave species, was especially important to this group. Parts of the plant are edible, and the Upland Yuma wove the leaves into beautiful baskets.

The Upland Yuma were made up of several subgroups, including the Havasupai *(HAH vuh SOO py)*, the Hualapai *(WAH luh py)*, and the Yavapai *(YAV uh py* or *YAH vuh py)*. Like the River Yuma, the Havasupai and Hualapai lived by cultivating gardens and hunting and gathering. The Yavapai relied primarily on hunting and gathering. The Havasupai lived in Havasu Canyon, a side canyon off of the Grand Canyon. The Hualapai lived to the south and west of this area. The Yavapai lived to the south.

▲ A Havasupai storyteller dressed in traditional clothing and face paint carries ceremonial items like those used by his ancestors. He might be acting out a legend about the tribe's creation or even a tale designed to teach youngsters how to behave.

NEW HOMES

Although many Yuma and Mohave now live on **reservations,** tribal leaders continue to place a strong emphasis on keeping traditions alive. One way they do this is by hosting or by attending powwows. A powwow is a gathering of Indian people and tribes. Although powwows were not a Mohave tradition, every year the tribe hosts one on its reservation. Members of many different tribes travel to the reservation to celebrate and share traditional dances, costumes, and customs.

THE PEOPLE CONTINUE

Ancestral Puebloans and some Mogollon **migrated** to settle along the upper Rio Grande in central New Mexico and also in northeastern Arizona and western New Mexico. Their influence can be easily seen in the **pueblos** that dominated these areas. These pueblos are considered to fall into two groups. The western pueblos (in western New Mexico and northeastern Arizona) were divided into **clans**, with children belonging to the clans of their mothers. The eastern pueblos (along the upper Rio Grande) were divided into **moieties**, such as the Winter moiety and the Summer moiety. Each group was responsible for the activities that took place during its season.

▲ Residents of the Acoma Pueblo continue to create traditional Pueblo crafts, including pottery that is valued by collectors around the world. Preserving traditional crafts is one way modern Indians maintain connection with their ancestors.

People of the Pueblos

During historic times (the period since the first contact with Europeans in the 1500's), Pueblo villages were generally populated by about 200 people. The multistory dwellings were built in tiers. The roof of each apartment was a plaza for the apartment above. Like their ancestors, families used these outdoor spaces for preparing food, making pottery, and storing dried food and firewood.

These settlements are not the only link between the historic Pueblo and their ancestors. Like Ancestral Puebloans, the Pueblo were mostly farmers who grew corn, pumpkins, melons, beans, and squash. After contact with the Spanish, they began to grow wheat and a variety of fruits and to keep horses, sheep, and cattle. The women also continued to make the beautiful pottery that is prized by collectors worldwide. Today, 19 pueblos still survive in New Mexico.

A CITY IN THE CLOUDS

The Acoma Pueblo in New Mexico, established in the 1100's, is the oldest inhabited city in the United States. Also known as "Sky City," Acoma sits atop a 357-foot- (109-meter-) high **mesa**. The only way in or out of the village is to climb up or down steps carved into the sandstone hundreds of years ago.

GLOSSARY

archaeologist A scientist who studies the remains of past human cultures.

artifact An object or the remains of an object, such as a tool, made by people in the past.

artisan A person skilled in some industry or trade.

atlatl A spear-throwing device once used by many Indian groups.

clan A group of people who are related through a common ancestor.

culture A society's arts, beliefs, customs, institutions, inventions, language, technology, and values.

dendrochronology A dating method based on studying the growth rings of trees.

desert varnish A glossy coating of certain chemicals found on rocks and pebbles after long exposure in desert regions.

domesticate To gain the ability to plant and grow specific crops, rather than simply gathering wild plants; or, to tame animals so they can be kept or raised.

equinox Either of the two moments each year when the sun appears directly above Earth's equator. During an equinox, all places on Earth receive approximately 12 hours of sunlight.

excavate To uncover or unearth by digging, especially used of archaeological sites.

geoglyph A huge etching made on the desert floor.

hunter-gatherer A person who hunts, fishes, and picks wild plants for food.

intaglio See **geoglyph.**

irrigation Supplying land with water using ditches or other artificial means.

kiva A structure, often built totally or partially underground, used for religious ceremonies.

loom A machine used for making cloth.

magma Molten rock.

mano A stone used for grinding grain.

masonry Stonework or brickwork.

matrilineal Tracing family relationships and ancestry through the mother's side.

mesa An isolated, flat-topped hill.

metate A rough stone with a flat or bowl-shaped surface.

midden A refuse heap.

migrate To move from one place to another.

moiety Two sections of a single society; each half is a moiety. Clans in certain Indian groups were divided into moieties.

nomadic Moving from place to place in search of food.

observatory A place used for watching the stars and sky.

obsidian A natural glass formed when hot lava flows onto the surface of Earth and cools quickly.

ornament A decorative accessory.

paho A prayer stick, usually carved from wood and often decorated with feathers, turquoise, and carved figures.

Paleo-Indians A term for some of the earliest known human inhabitants of the Americas who lived from about 13,500 to 8,000 years ago.

patrilineal Tracing family relationships and ancestry through the father's side.

petroglyph A rock carving, usually a picture or symbol.

pictogram A picture symbol in certain writing systems that could be used to stand for an idea, a sound, or a name.

pit house An ancient house style, made by digging a hole in the ground and constructing a shelter over the pit.

poncho A cloth with a slit in the middle, worn as a cloak.

potsherd A broken piece of pottery.

pueblo An Indian village built of adobe and stone that resembled modern apartment buildings.

radiocarbon dating A method used to determine the age of an object by measuring the amount of radiocarbon—or carbon 14—left in it.

ramada An open-sided shelter.

rancheria A temporary Patayan village.

reservation An area of land set aside and reserved for American Indians.

ritual A solemn or important act or ceremony, often religious in nature.

sacred Holy.

seminomadic Partly nomadic; not living in the same place year-round.

sipapu An opening in the floor of a kiva through which supernatural beings were believed to travel.

slip Wet, fine clay used in pottery.

solstice One of the two moments each year when the sun appears in the sky at either its northernmost or southern-most position. The solstices take place in June and December.

supernatural Above or beyond what is natural.

wattle and daub A building material made of reeds and clay.

yucca cordage Ropes or cords made from the leaves of the yucca plant.

ADDITIONAL RESOURCES

Books

The Anasazi
by William W. Lace (Lucent Books, 2005)

The Anasazi Culture at Mesa Verde
by Sabrina Crewe and Dale Anderson
(Gareth Stevens, 2003)

The Lost World of the Anasazi: Exploring the Mysteries of the Chaco Canyon
by Peter Lourie (Boyds Mills Press, 2003)

101 Questions About Ancient Indians of the Southwest
by David Grant Noble (Southwest Parks and Monuments Association, 1998)

Stories on Stone: Rock Art Images from the Ancient Ones
by Jennifer Owings Dewey
(University of New Mexico Press, 2003)

Web Sites

http://sipapu.gsu.edu

http://www.blm.gov/co/st/en/fo/ahc/who_were_the_anasazi.html

http://www.cavecreekmuseum.org

http://www.nps.gov/cagr/forkids/parkfun.htm

http://www.puebloindian.com

INDEX

Acknowledgments

The Art Archive: 37 (Mesa Verde National Park Museum/Mireille Vautier); Bridgeman Art Library: 32 (Peter Newark Western Americana), 48 (Museum of Fine Arts, Houston, Texas); Corbis: 7 (Natalie Tepper/Arcaid), 9, 12, 17, 38, 49 (Richard A. Cooke), 10, 22 (Buddy Mays), 13 (Dewitt Jones), 14, 31, 43 (George H. H. Huey), 16, 30 (Scott T. Smith), 18, 36, 51 (David Muench), 19 (Gordon Whitten), 21 (Steven Clevenger), 27 (Jan Butchofsky-Houser), 29, 40 (DLILLC), 34, 50, 52, 55 (Tom Bean), 42 (Greg Probst), 47 (Yann Arthus-Bertrand), 53 (Erich Schlegel/Dallas Morning News), 54 (no photographer credited), 57 (Catherine Karnow), 58 (Danny Lehman), 59 (Adam Woolfitt); Library of Congress: 56; Shutterstock: 4 (Dan Breckwoldt), 35 (Douglas Knight), 39 (Darla Hallmark), 46 (John Bell); Topfoto: 23 (Charles Walker); Werner Forman Archive: 1, 8, 11, 24, 44, 45 (Arizona State Museum), 5, 15 (Maxwell Museum of Anthropology, Albuquerque, NM), 20, 25 (Museum of Northern Arizona), 33 (Mesa Verde National Park Museum).

Cover image: Shutterstock (Zack Frank)
Back cover image: Shutterstock (Joop Snijder, Jr.)